DATE DUE   APR   2012

Pebble® Plus

Cool Sports Facts

Cool Pro Wrestling Facts

by Angie Peterson Kaelberer

Consulting Editor: Gail Saunders-Smith, PhD

Consultant: Mike Johnson
Writer, PWInsider.com

CAPSTONE PRESS
a capstone imprint

Pebble Plus is published by Capstone Press,
151 Good Counsel Drive, P.O. Box 669, Mankato, Minnesota 56002.
www.capstonepub.com

Books published by Capstone Press are manufactured with paper
containing at least 10 percent post-consumer waste.

Library of Congress Cataloging-in-Publication Data
Kaelberer, Angie Peterson.
 Cool pro wrestling facts / by Angie Peterson Kaelberer.
     p. cm. — (Pebble plus. Cool sports facts)
 Includes bibliographical references and index.
 Summary: "Simple text and full-color photos illustrate facts about the history, moves, props, and records of
pro wrestling"—Provided by publisher.
  ISBN 978-1-4296-5305-3 (library binding)
  ISBN 978-1-4296-6205-5 (paperback)
 1. Wrestling—Juvenile literature. I. Title. II. Series.
GV1195.3.K34 2011
796.812—dc22   2010028900

Editorial Credits

Katy Kudela, editor; Kyle Grenz, designer; Eric Gohl, media researcher; Laura Manthe, production specialist

Photo Credits

AP Images/Erik S. Lesser, 21
Getty Images Inc./Ethan Miller, 5; George Napolitano, 7; LatinContent/Jam Media/Alfredo Lopez, cover, 15;
     Stone/John Eder, cover (ring), back cover, 1; WireImage/Bob Levey, 17
Globe Photos, 9, 11
Newscom/Icon SMI/Cityfiles/Alexandre Pona, 19
Zuma Press/Icon SMI/Tom 'Mo' Moschella, 13

Note to Parents and Teachers

The Cool Sports Facts series supports national social studies standards related to people, places,
and culture. This book describes and illustrates pro wrestling. The images support early readers
in understanding the text. The repetition of words and phrases helps early readers learn new
words. This book also introduces early readers to subject-specific vocabulary words, which are
defined in the Glossary section. Early readers may need assistance to read some words and to
use the Table of Contents, Glossary, Read More, Internet Sites, and Index sections of the book.

Printed in the United States of America in North Mankato, Minnesota.

042011   006171R

Table of Contents

Author's Note:
Before entering the ring, pro wrestlers train for months or even years. They learn how to use props and do moves without seriously hurting themselves or their opponents. The wrestling props and moves shown in this book should never be tried at home.

Ready to Rumble!

Slam! Two pro wrestlers
battle in the ring.
Around the world,
500 million people watch
the WWE match on TV.

WWE stands for World Wrestling Entertainment.

Cool History

Most pro wrestling matches last
about 10 minutes.
Some last only a few seconds.
The longest match ever
lasted five hours.

Cool Props

A folding chair isn't
just for sitting.
It also comes in handy
against opponents
during a match!

Inside the ring,

pro wrestlers sometimes

throw opponents

through tables. Ouch!

11

Cool Moves

Pro wrestlers need to be strong. In a powerbomb, a wrestler lifts another wrestler on his shoulders. Smash! The opponent falls back onto the mat.

The shooting star press

is full of danger. A pro wrestler

jumps off the ring ropes

then backflips. Splat!

The wrestler pins his opponent.

A chokeslam is an exciting

way to end a match.

A pro wrestler grabs an

opponent by the neck and

slams him to the mat.

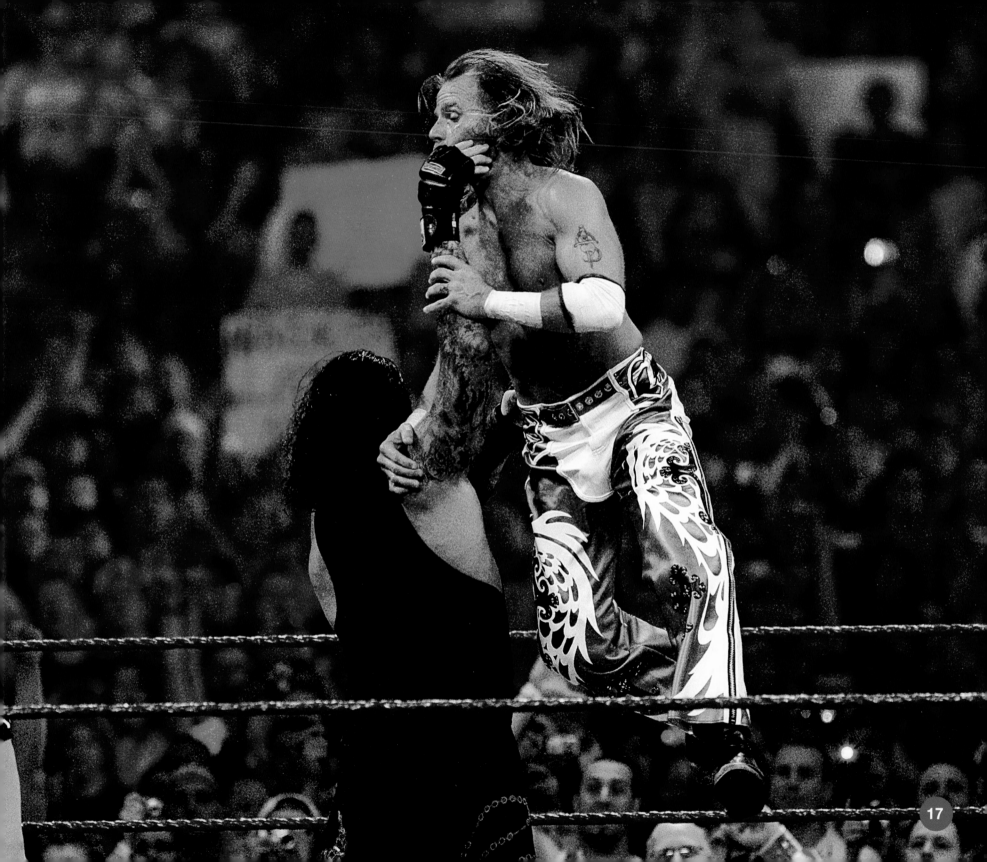

Cool Records

Undertaker has been a top pro wrestler since 1990. He has never been beaten at WrestleMania.

Bill Goldberg has the longest winning streak in pro wrestling. He won 173 matches from September 1997 to December 1998.

Glossary

mat—a large, thick floor pad used to protect wrestlers and other athletes

match—a game or sporting competition

opponent—a person who competes against another person in a game or contest

pin—to hold someone firmly in position

ring—the area in which a wrestling or boxing match takes place

winning streak—an unbroken series of winning matches

WrestleMania—the biggest televised event in pro wrestling

Read More

Nemeth, Jason D. *Randy Orton.* Stars of Pro Wrestling. Mankato, Minn.: Capstone Press, 2010.

O'Shei, Tim. *Undertaker.* Stars of Pro Wrestling. Mankato, Minn.: Capstone Press, 2010.

Internet Sites

FactHound offers a safe, fun way to find Internet sites related to this book. All of the sites on FactHound have been researched by our staff.

Here's all you do:

Visit *www.facthound.com*

Type in this code: 9781429653053

Super-cool stuff! Check out projects, games and lots more at www.capstonekids.com

Index

Word Count: 179

Grade: 1

Early-Intervention Level: 20